THIS OR THAT? History Edition

Building the
TRANSCONTINENTAL RAILROAD

A This or That Debate

by **Jessica Rusick**

CAPSTONE PRESS
a capstone imprint

T0019013

Capstone Captivate is published by Capstone Press, an imprint of Capstone.
1710 Roe Crest Drive
North Mankato, Minnesota 56003
www.capstonepub.com

Library of Congress Cataloging-in-Publication Data is available on the Library of Congress website.
ISBN: 978-1-4966-8394-6 (library binding)
ISBN: 978-1-4966-8792-0 (paperback)
ISBN: 978-1-4966-8445-5 (eBook PDF)

Summary: In the 1860s, the U.S. government hired two companies to build a railroad across the United States. This railway made travel across the country easier. Test your decision-making skills with this or that questions related to building the railroad!

Image Credits
Flickr: Internet Archive Book Images, 8, 9, 17, 19, 21, 23, 26; Library of Congress: Edwin Ferry Johnson, Cover (map), Waud, Alfred R. (Alfred Rudolph) 1828-1891, artist, 16; National Park Service: Cover (train), 3, 14; North Wind Picture Archives: 11; NYPL: Gardner; Alexander, 6; Shutterstock: Breck P. Kent, 4–5, Chaikom, 12, Darin Burks, Cover (railroad spikes), Everett Historical, 7, 22, grafvision, 25, rook76, 24, Sarfoto, Cover (hammer), Stephen Rees, 30, vellot, 13, Zack Frank, Cover (camp), Zoran Milic, 5 (map); Stanford Libraries: Alfred A. Hart, 15, 20; Wikimedia Commons: 29, B&H, illustrator, sketch by Joesph Becker (1841-1910), 28, Beinecke Rare Book and Manuscript Library, 18, Robert N. Dennis collection of stereoscopic views/New York Public Library, 10, Yale University Libraries, 27

Design Elements: Edwin Ferry Johnson/Library of Congress

Editorial Credits
Editor: Rebecca Felix; Designers: Aruna Rangarajan & Tamara JM Peterson; Production Specialist: Tori Abraham

All internet sites appearing in back matter were available and accurate when this book was sent to press.

A PROJECT LIKE NO OTHER

In 1862, the U.S. government tasked two companies to build a railroad across the United States. Union Pacific Railroad Company would start laying track in Nebraska. Central Pacific Railroad Company would start in California. The tracks would meet in the middle.

Tens of thousands of workers built the railroad. Hundreds got hurt or died from accidents and disease. The railroad also affected native peoples. It displaced many tribes' way of life.

On May 10, 1869, the tracks met in Utah. The Transcontinental Railroad was complete. It was now easier than ever to travel across the United States.

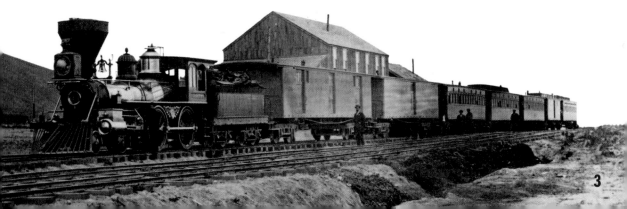

HOW TO USE THIS BOOK

What if you had been a worker on the Transcontinental Railroad? What choices would you have made along the way? Do you think you would have survived?

This book is full of questions that relate to the Transcontinental Railroad. Some are questions real people had to face. The questions are followed by details to help you come to a decision.

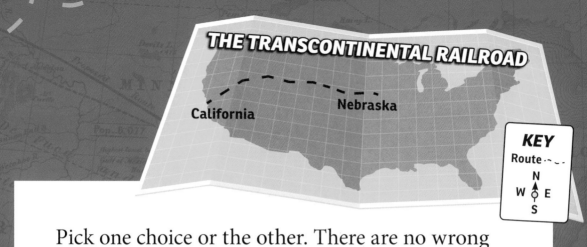

THE TRANSCONTINENTAL RAILROAD

California   Nebraska

KEY
Route ·---·
N
W ⊙ E
S

Pick one choice or the other. There are no wrong answers! But just like the workers, you should think carefully about your decisions.

Are you ready? Turn the page to pick this or that!

Would you choose . . .

THIS

To work for the
UNION PACIFIC RAILROAD company?

- ➤ face tornadoes and dust storms
- ➤ make more money, but must pay extra fees
- ➤ sleep in crowded railway cars

Union Pacific (UP) workers started their route on flat land. Here, they were more likely to face tornadoes and dust storms. UP workers made up to $4 a day. But unlike Central Pacific (CP) workers, they had to pay for their **board**. UP workers slept in railway cars. Each car was 85 feet (26 meters) long by 10 feet (3 m) wide. Up to 200 workers stayed in one car.

To work for the
CENTRAL PACIFIC RAILROAD company?

- ➤ work in the freezing Sierra Nevada mountains
- ➤ build lots of tunnels
- ➤ stay in tents

CP workers laid track through rugged land on the railroad's route. This included the Sierra Nevada mountains in California. Workers **chiseled** and blasted through rock to build tunnels. They also faced blizzards and **avalanches**. Even in these cold conditions, workers stayed in tents. They made up to $31 a month.

Would you choose . . .

THIS

To BUILD SNOW SHEDS?

➤ build sheds to protect train tracks

➤ work in freezing temperatures

➤ must be rebuilt often

Snow sheds were roofed structures built to protect mountain tracks from snow. Workers built the sheds into mountainsides. They put up 15-foot- (5-m-) wide wooden planks in freezing temperatures. Tracklaying cars hauled these supplies to the workers. But the cars could throw sparks that burned down the sheds. This meant the sheds had to be constantly rebuilt.

To SURVEY LAND?

> explore unknown, possibly dangerous land

> travel without maps

> find path through mountains

Surveyors traveled west to find the best path for the railroad. They had to explore more than 2,000 miles (3,219 kilometers) of land, sometimes without maps. They faced dangerous wild animals, bad weather, and difficult landscapes. Some had to find routes through mountains or around large bodies of water.

THIS

To be a
GRADER?

> make even path for railroad

> lots of digging in dirt

> paid the least of any worker

A grader's job was to make the land flat and even. That way, other workers could lay track. Graders had to flatten hills and fill in ditches. That meant digging a lot of dirt. Graders shoveled some dirt into wheelbarrows and carted it away. Other dirt was used as fill. Graders got paid the least out of any railroad worker.

To be a TRACKLAYER?

➤ build the railroad

➤ lots of heavy lifting

➤ repeated motion makes muscles sore

Tracklayers built the railroad. First, they laid horizontal wooden bars called ties. These weighed up to 200 pounds (91 kilograms)! Tracklayers laid pieces of 60-pound (27-kg) metal rail on top of the ties. They attached the rails to the ties by hammering in big metal spikes. Tracklayers had to be strong. They could easily get sore from lifting and hammering.

THIS

To get sick with
DYSENTERY?

➤ from drinking bad water

➤ causes vomiting and diarrhea

➤ can cause death

Many workers drank water from nearby streams or rivers. This water was dirty with trash and animal poop. It could also hold dangerous **bacteria**. These tiny living things can cause sicknesses such as dysentery. Dysentery made workers **vomit** and have **diarrhea**. This caused weakness and **dehydration**. In bad cases, dysentery could kill.

OR THAT?

To get sick with SCURVY?

➤ from poor diet

➤ causes weakness

➤ can be deadly, especially when combined with other illnesses

Many railroad workers ate foods like boiled meat and potatoes. As a result, workers suffered from scurvy. This disease happens when people do not get enough vitamin C from fruits and vegetables. Scurvy causes weakness and bleeding gums. It can also make people's teeth fall out. When combined with other illnesses, scurvy could kill.

13

Would you choose . . .

THIS

To stay in a
UP RAILROAD CAMP?

- ➤ food provided
- ➤ better shelter
- ➤ more likely to get sick

UP Railroad workers slept in train cars. The railroad company also provided food. However, the food was not nutritious. Because of this, workers in this camp were more likely to get sick from lack of nutrition. UP workers also got sick from drinking bad water. They drank from nearby streams. This water was dirty and caused sickness.

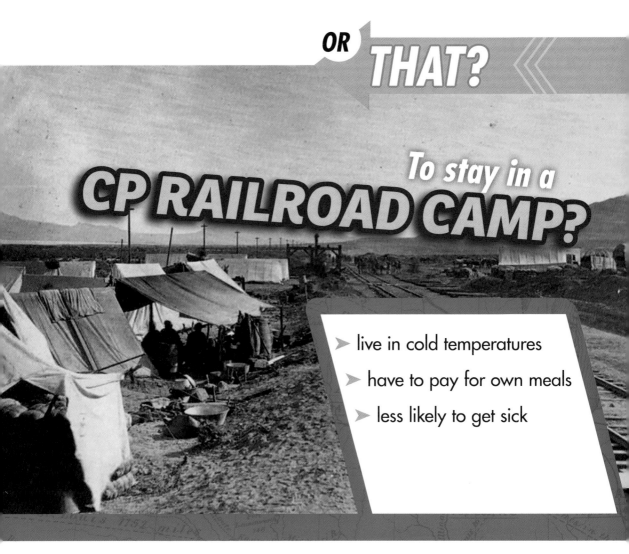

To stay in a CP RAILROAD CAMP?

> live in cold temperatures

> have to pay for own meals

> less likely to get sick

CP Railroad workers lived in tents in the cold Sierra Nevada mountains. Tents did not provide much warmth or protection from bad weather. CP workers had to pay for their own food. However, this often meant they ate healthier meals. Healthier meals meant CP workers received more nutrition. This made them less likely to get sick.

Would you choose . . .

THIS

To blast through rock using
NITROGLYCERIN?

> more powerful

> more dangerous

> harder to ship

Nitroglycerin is an explosive liquid. It is powerful. Workers used it to blast through rock twice as quickly than with black powder. However, nitroglycerin was unstable. When shipped, it could blow up and kill people. Because of this, most nitroglycerin was made on-site. Workers were always at risk of unexpected explosions.

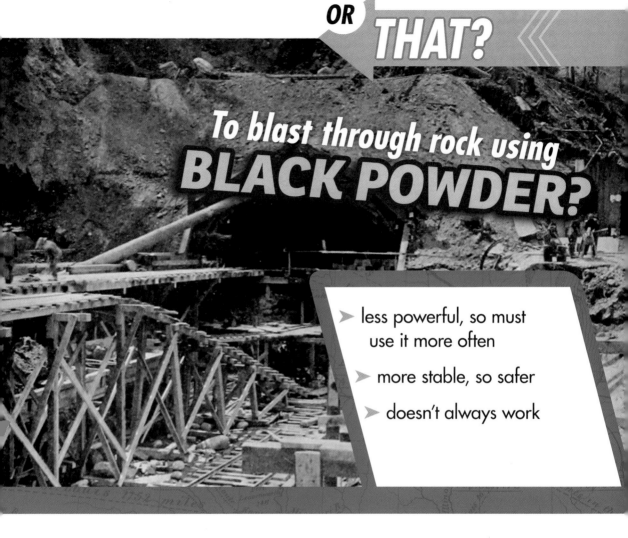

THAT?

To blast through rock using BLACK POWDER?

➤ less powerful, so must use it more often

➤ more stable, so safer

➤ doesn't always work

Black powder was not as unstable as nitroglycerin. But it was still dangerous. Black powder was also not as powerful. It took workers twice as long to blast through rock. This meant they had to spend more time around potentially deadly explosions. Black powder also didn't work when wet, so using it in rain or snow was not always successful.

THIS

To help build a
BRIDGE?

- work high up
- strong winds
- could fall to your death

Workers built wooden bridges across large streams and rivers. Some bridges were hundreds of feet high. Winds caused them to sway as they were being built. Workers steadied the bridges with ropes and chains. Workers who fell from bridges could drown in the water below. In some cases, the fall itself could kill them.

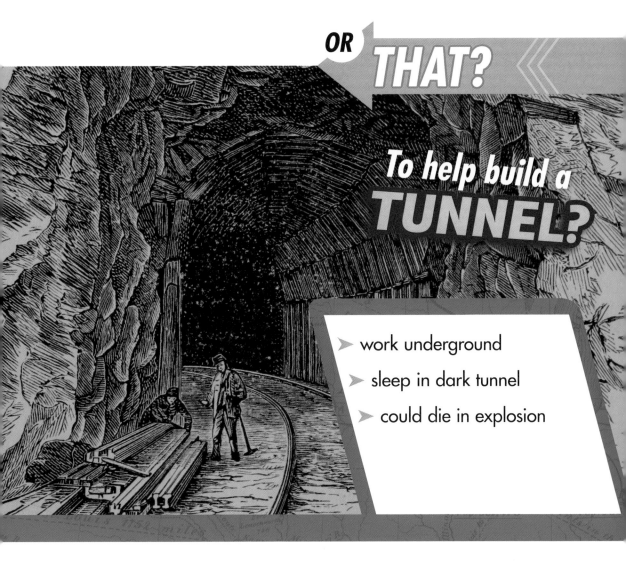

To help build a
TUNNEL?

➤ work underground

➤ sleep in dark tunnel

➤ could die in explosion

Workers built tunnels by exploding through rock with nitroglycerin or black powder. They packed the explosive inside rock holes. Then they lit a fuse and ran. If the fuse was too short, workers could get caught in explosions and die. Workers spent eight-hour shifts in the dark tunnels. Some workers even slept in the tunnels. This saved time going back and forth from camp.

Would you choose . . .

THIS

To
BLAST A PATH
in Cape Horn?

> must blast through mountain rock

> lowered down from high spot

> could be hurt or killed in explosion

Cape Horn is in California. There, workers had to carve space for the track into a steep mountain face. Workers were lowered in baskets from cliffs. They chiseled holes in the rock and filled them with black powder. The workers were yanked up before the powder exploded, but not always in time. Hundreds were killed in explosions.

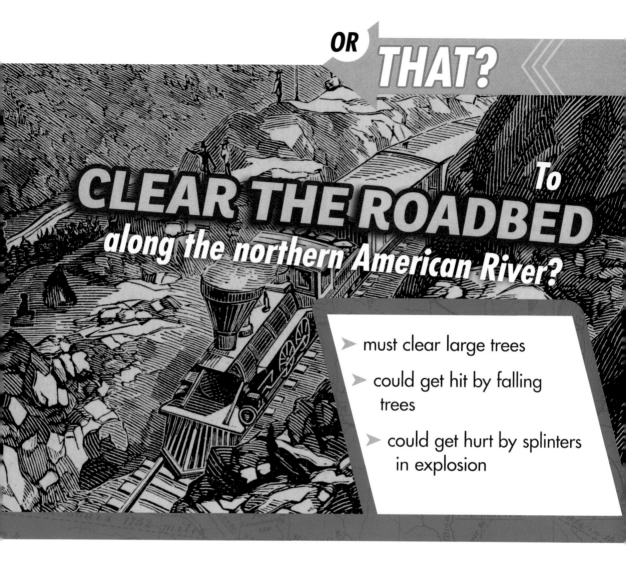

To **CLEAR THE ROADBED** along the northern American River?

> must clear large trees
> could get hit by falling trees
> could get hurt by splinters in explosion

Workers had to clear the land before laying track. One of the hardest spots to clear was along the northern American River in California. Here, trees were hundreds of feet tall! Workers were in danger of getting hit by chopped trees as they fell. The men used explosives to blast large stumps out of the ground. They could get hit with giant splinters from these explosions.

THIS

To work in the
DESERT DURING SUMMER?

- ➤ high temperatures
- ➤ could pass out from heat
- ➤ might get paid extra

Desert temperatures could reach 120 degrees Fahrenheit (49 degrees Celsius). Workers who didn't drink enough water could pass out from the heat. They could also get **heatstroke**. This happens when a person's body overheats. In bad cases, heatstroke can cause organ damage and death. However, some workers were paid more to work in hot weather.

To work in the
MOUNTAINS DURING WINTER?

- freezing cold
- must dig through snow before starting work
- could die in avalanche

Workers also laid track in cold, snowy mountains. They had to work in several feet of snow. Some had to dig snow tunnels to get to the areas they were working on. Workers slept in these tunnels. Avalanches were also a danger. Workers died when they were buried in snow. Most bodies weren't found until after the snow melted.

THIS

To serve as a
RAILROAD DOCTOR?

- ➤ treat railroad workers
- ➤ must see gross injuries
- ➤ hard to treat patients in dirty conditions

Railroad doctors treated injured workers. They had to see many gross injuries, including broken bones and crushed fingers. Workers could also be badly hurt in explosions. In some cases, doctors had to **amputate** body parts. Doctors did not have clean offices to work in. This made it difficult to keep wounds clean.

To serve as a
RAILROAD BLACKSMITH?

> fix railroad tools

> work over hot fire

> dirty from soot

Blacksmiths fixed iron tools for railroad workers. This was hot, sweaty work. Blacksmiths worked over fires that reached up to 2,102 degrees Fahrenheit (1,150°C)! These workers were always at risk of burning themselves. They would also get dirty from **soot** and breathe in dangerous fumes from the smoke.

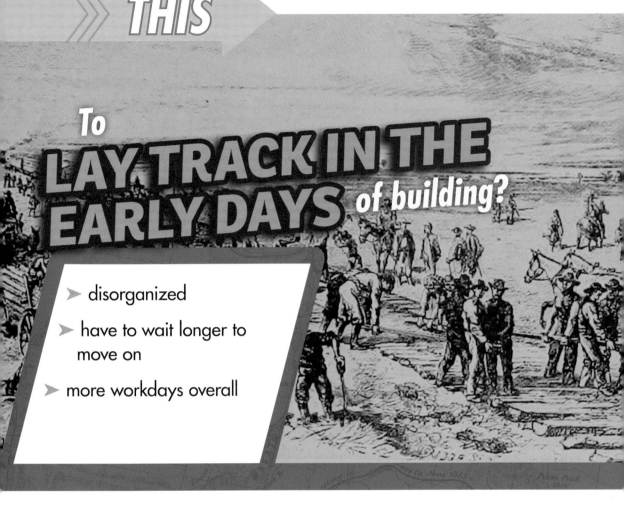

Would you choose . . .

THIS

To LAY TRACK IN THE EARLY DAYS of building?

- ➤ disorganized
- ➤ have to wait longer to move on
- ➤ more workdays overall

In the early days of building, groups of workers built one piece of track at a time. Each worker did multiple jobs. Then everyone moved to the next piece when that portion was complete. Workers laid about 1 mile (1.6 km) of track a day. This meant less walking each day. However, it also meant there would be more workdays overall.

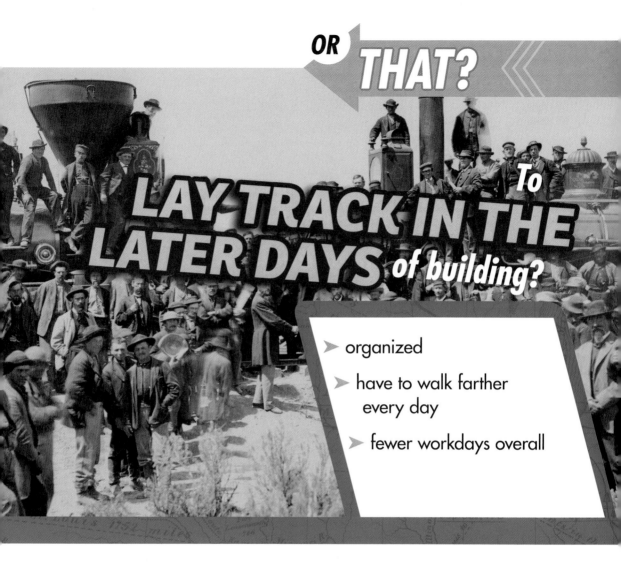

To LAY TRACK IN THE LATER DAYS of building?

- organized
- have to walk farther every day
- fewer workdays overall

Later on, companies moved to assembly-line track laying. Every worker had a certain job. Each worker moved to the next piece of track after it was done. This allowed the companies to lay more track than ever. In 1869, the CP Railroad laid 10 miles (16 km) of track in one day. Workers walked farther each day than before. But they accomplished more in fewer workdays.

Would you choose . . .

THIS

To STOP STRIKING
after being threatened?

- get to go back to normal food rations
- only lose a little money
- stopping early makes strike less effective

In 1867, CP Railroad workers went on **strike** for better hours and pay. Bosses cut the workers' food **rations**. They also said workers would lose a month's wages if they didn't get back to work. These threats made many workers stop striking within a week. But strikes work best when there are enough people to get the bosses to listen. Going back to work hurt the strike's chance of being successful.

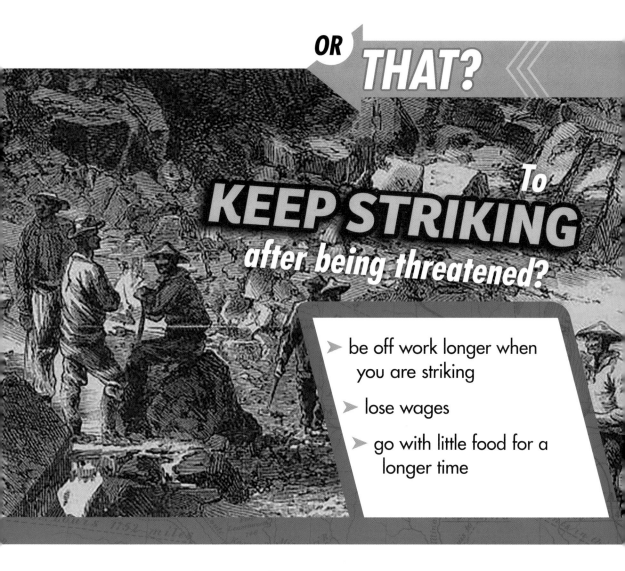

To **KEEP STRIKING** after being threatened?

➤ be off work longer when you are striking

➤ lose wages

➤ go with little food for a longer time

Some workers kept striking. This meant going even longer with little food. These workers also lost an entire month's wages. In the end, the strike wasn't successful. The remaining strikers returned to work within a few more days, after their boss threatened to physically hurt them. But those who held out got the satisfaction of fighting longer for what they believed in.

LIGHTNING ROUND

Would you choose to . . .

➤ play cards or sing songs to relax after a long day of work?

➤ break an arm or break a leg in a landslide?

➤ buy dried fish or tomatoes as a special treat?

➤ injure your knee or back while laying track?

➤ visit a prairie dog colony or hunt for buffalo on a day off?

➤ fill a hole with dirt or cart dirt out of the hole?

➤ cook camp meals or care for camp's wagon animals?

➤ send railroad wages home to family or keep them as savings?

➤ attend the ceremony celebrating the start of railroad building or for the completion of the railroad?

amputate (AM-pyuh-tate)—to cut off someone's limb, usually because it is diseased or damaged

avalanche (AV-uh-lanch)—a large mass of snow, ice, or earth that suddenly falls down a mountainside

bacterium (bak-TEER-ee-uhm)—a microscopic, single-celled living thing that can either be useful or harmful

board (BORD)—meals provided to people paying to stay somewhere

chisel (CHIZ-uhl)—to carefully cut something to form it into a desired shape

dehydration (dee-HYE-dray-shun)—lacking enough water in your body for normal functioning

diarrhea (dye-uh-REE-uh)—a condition in which normally solid waste from your body becomes liquid

heatstroke (HEET-strohk)—a life-threatening condition that results from prolonged exposure to high temperature

ration (RASH-uhn)—a limited amount or share

soot (SUT)—black powder produced when coal or wood is burned

strike (STRIKE)—to refuse to work until an employer meets certain demands

vomit (VAH-mit)—to bring up food from the stomach and expel it through the mouth

READ MORE

Bailey, Budd. *The Transcontinental Railroad.* New York: Cavendish Square Publishing, 2018.

Harasymiw, Therese. *The Transcontinental Railroad: Connecting a Nation.* New York: Lucent Press, 2018.

Otfinoski, Steven. *Building the Transcontinental Railroad: An Interactive Engineering Adventure.* Mankato, MN: Capstone Press, 2015.

INTERNET SITES

DK Find Out!—History of Trains
https://www.dkfindout.com/us/transportation/history-trains/

Ducksters—Westward Expansion: First Transcontinental Railroad
https://www.ducksters.com/history/westward_expansion/first
_transcontinental_railroad.php

Social Studies for Kids—The Transcontinental Railroad
https://www.socialstudiesforkids.com/articles/ushistory
/transcontinentalrailroad.htm